Nonprofit Quick Guide™

Seven Simple Strategies to Creating a Wildly Successful Fundraising Program

Joanne Oppelt, MHA
Linda Lysakowski, ACFRE

Nonprofit Quick Guide: Seven Simple Strategies to Creating a Wildly Successful Fundraising Program

One of the **Nonprofit Quick Guide**™ series

Published by Joanne Oppelt Consulting, LLC

Copyright © 2020 by Joanne Oppelt and Linda Lysakowski

ISBN Print Book: 978-1-951978-02-0

13 12 11 10 9 8 7 6 5 4 3 2 1

Printed in the United States of America

About the Authors

JOANNE OPPELT, MHA

Joanne, principal of Joanne Oppelt Consulting, LLC, is a seasoned rainmaker with a distinguished track record of success. During her twenty-five-plus years working in the nonprofit arena, she built or rebuilt successful fundraising departments at every stop, helping her organizations grow capacity and more effectively fulfill their missions.

She has held positions from grantwriter to executive director at the nonprofits Community Access Unlimited, Caring Contact: A Listening Community, Family to Family Network of New Jersey, Christian Healthcare Center, March of Dimes Central New Jersey, Prevent Child Abuse New Jersey, and Maternal and Family Health Services. Her extensive background in a variety of work roles and organizations enables her to understand the realities and challenges nonprofit practitioners face–both internally and externally. Her success at every stop positions her to help any nonprofit, whether through her books, trainings, coaching, or consulting practice

Joanne is the author of four books and co-author of four. She has taught at Kean University as an Adjunct Professor in its graduate program. She is also a highly sought-after speaker and presenter.

Joanne holds a master's degree in health administration from Wilkes University, where she graduated with distinction. Her bachelor's degree is in education, with a minor in psychology.

LINDA LYSAKOWSKI, ACFRE

Linda is one of approximately one hundred professionals worldwide to hold the Advanced Certified Fundraising Executive designation. Linda is the author of ten nonfiction books and a contributing author, co-editor, or co-author of seventeen others. She has also written six books in the fiction realm.

Linda has more than thirty years in the development field. She worked for a university and a museum before starting her own consulting firm. In her twenty-five years as a philanthropic consultant, Linda has managed capital campaigns that have raised more than $50 million. She's helped hundreds of nonprofit organizations achieve their development goals and trained more than forty thousand development professionals in most of the fifty states of the United States as well as in Canada, Mexico, Egypt, and Bermuda.

She served on the Association of Fundraising Philanthropy (AFP) Foundation for Philanthropy Board and on the Professional Advancement Division for AFP. She is a past president of the Eastern Pennsylvania and Sierra (Nevada) AFP chapters. She received the Outstanding Fundraiser of the Year award from the Eastern Pennsylvania, Las Vegas, and Sierra (Nevada) chapters of AFP, was honored with the Barbara Marion Award for Outstanding Service to AFP, and received the Lifetime Achievement Award from the Las Vegas AFP chapter.

Linda is a graduate of Alvernia University with majors in banking and finance as well as theology/philosophy, and a minor in communications. As a graduate of AFP's Faculty Training Academy, she is a Master Teacher.

Dedication

This book is dedicated to all the fundraisers and executive directors trying to thrive.

Contents

Chapter One 1
Improving Income by Decreasing Costs

Chapter Two 5
What to Consider When Developing Your Fundraising Plan

Chapter Three 11
Understanding and Reaching Individual Donors

Chapter Four 21
Making the Most of Your Grants Planning

Chapter Five 29
Getting the Most Out of Corporate Contributions

Chapter Six 33
Planning for the Success of Your Fundraising Events: Income,
Impact, Costs, and Benefits

Chapter Seven 37
Creating a Profitable Nonprofit Fundraising Budget and Calendar

Chapter Eight 43
Bringing It All Together

Chapter One

Improving Income by Decreasing Costs

E very executive director, board member, and fundraising professional we know wants to increase revenues to their nonprofit organization. The question they ask is, "What fundraising strategy will generate the most income for my nonprofit?"

To measure increasing income, we mean increasing net income, not gross income. Gross income is total revenues. Net income is revenues minus costs. There are two factors involved in increasing net income: increasing incomes *and* reducing costs. Both are important. It doesn't matter how much money you raise if your costs to raise it exceed your revenues. High gross income means nothing if net income is a loss.

The fastest and least expensive way to increase net income is to reduce costs. According to the Fundraising Effectiveness Project, the cost, including labor, to raise one dollar through grant writing is $0.20; $0.25 through business giving; and $0.25 through existing individual donors. It costs $1.50, on average, to acquire a new donor through direct mail, including labor. The average cost to raise a dollar through a fundraising event is $0.50, *not* including labor. If your costs to raise one dollar are higher than average, you may want to look at where you can reduce costs.

In addition to your direct fundraising expenses, look at your fundraising operational costs: your banking fees, credit card fees, and donor management software costs, among others. Then look at your organizational general operating costs, for example, office supplies and janitorial costs. To realize increased agency net income, you may want your fundraising strategy to include negotiating with vendors to reduce your fundraising and organizational operating costs.

An often-overlooked way of reducing fundraising costs is by improving your donor retention rate. We talk at length about retaining donors in the Nonprofit Quick Guide *How to Find New Donors and Get Them to Give to Again.* According to the Fundraising Effectiveness Project, the average donor retention rate is 46 percent. That means that of every hundred donors a nonprofit gains, it loses sixty-four. And if it costs more than a dollar to realize each dollar gained, your heavy emphasis on donor recruitment is costing you more than you are realizing in income. Since it costs more to acquire new donors than retain current ones, a shift in strategy from a heavy emphasis on new donor acquisition to a heavy emphasis on current donor retention may well be the cost-beneficial way to improve fundraising performance.

Other costs that you can cut include those that are unnecessary or that have a poor return on investment. These types of costs may include a direct mail appeal to all your donors, if the majority probably responds better to email. Or that expensive ink on an event invitation when no one will really know the difference if you use a less expensive one. Or a fancy sit-down dinner when a cocktail gathering will do.

What costs *don't* you cut?

Don't cut anything that yields a good return on investment, for example, a software-based or online donor database. You might not need the most expensive one out there, but you do need a donor database that will do what you need it to do, like integrate your mailing, donor, and volunteer lists. Likewise, a foundation and grants database is a good investment, saving hours spent in grant research.

Sometimes training is seen as an optional expense. Not true. Studies show that fundraisers who receive more training yield better fundraising results. Those few hundred dollars your agency spends on networking events, conferences, and webinars may be helping you realize thousands of dollars in more efficient fundraising operations through improved fundraising techniques picked up during those networking and training experiences.

Another fundraising cost often considered frivolous is administrative support. Properly executing fundraising activities involves many administrative tasks. There are donations to enter and mailing lists to keep updated. There are reports to run. There are acknowledgment letters to be sent. There are invitations to design and send out. There are RSVP's to track. There may be seating charts or golf foursomes to create. There are supplies to order. There are name tags to make. There are grants to copy, including large attachments like IRS Form 990s and audits. If you're pursuing government contracts, there's even more paperwork. There are also phone

calls to field, questions to answer, and appointments to make. If you are also responsible for communications, you also have newsletters to format and email campaigns to manage. Administrative support is crucial to efficient fundraising operations. Look at it from a cost perspective. Who costs you more: a fundraising professional or an administrative assistant? How much money are you *not* making while your fundraising professional is engaged in administrative work?

Net, not gross, income is what counts. The most inexpensive and immediate way to improve fundraising income is to decrease costs. Improving your donor retention rate is one of the best ways to reduce fundraising costs and realize more net income. But don't cut expenses that increase productivity. Spending that yields a high return on investment is well worth the expense.

Wrapping It Up

◆ To raise the most money, look at net as opposed to gross income.

◆ The least expensive way to improve net income is to decrease costs.

◆ Consider reducing associated operating costs.

◆ Lower fundraising costs by improving your donor retention rate.

◆ Be careful what expenses you cut. Keep expenses that improve fundraising results.

Chapter Two

What to Consider When Developing Your Fundraising Plan

Nonprofits usually realize fundraising revenues through individual giving, foundation funding, corporate contributions, special events, and government contracts. What are the financial costs and benefits of implementing each fundraising technique?

Considerations for Raising Money from Individuals

According to *Giving USA* 2019, individuals make up the biggest piece of the fundraising pie, at 77 percent. The return on investment to raise one dollar through an existing donor is relatively low, although the costs to acquire new donors may result in a financial loss. You must, however, recruit new donors. Donor attrition will occur. Individual donors can be recruited and asked to give through your website, email campaign, direct mail campaign, social media posts, or face to face. The Nonprofit Quick Guide *How to Find New Donors and Get Them to Give to Again* discusses donor acquisition and retention in detail.

Your upfront costs to raise money from individuals include a donor management system and a way to accept credit cards. Before you start, you will want a donor recruitment plan, a donor retention plan, and training for your askers. Depending on how many ways you want to ask individuals, you may also need to optimize your website, invest in an email campaign system, and integrate fundraising messages into agency communications. After implementing an individual donation fundraising program, you will need someone to research donors, record the research, recruit the donors, implement the donor communication vehicles, track the response to the communications, answer questions when potential donors have questions, record donor interactions, receive donations, record the donations, write thank-you letters, refund donations when there is a problem, and report back to the donor the use of the donation.

Considerations for Raising Money through Foundations

Foundations make up 18 percent of the charitable giving pie. The average return on investment is very high. The way to ask for money from a foundation is by submitting a grant proposal.

To get started in grant writing, you need a foundation database search tool and a recordkeeping system. You will probably also need audited financial statements. You will need to research potential foundations, record the research, make a grants calendar, write the grant proposal, answer questions if the funder has any questions about the proposal, monitor and record funder responses, record donations and their purpose, write thank-you letters, monitor agency performance against grant promises, and write grant reports.

Considerations for Raising Money through the Business Community

Corporate contributions make up five percent of the charitable giving pie. The return on investment is relatively high. Businesses give through employee matching gift programs, employee volunteer programs, in-kind or non-monetary donations, outright gifts, sponsorships, employee donor advised funds, and corporate foundations.

Before approaching business donors, you will need a donor management system. You may also need your agency's financial statements. You will want to create sponsorship templates, a donor recruitment plan, and a donor retention plan. You will need to research potential companies, record the research, reach out to the contact, follow up with the contact, make the ask, monitor and record responses, record donations, and write thank-you letters. If giving is through a corporate foundation, you will need to write grant proposals, monitor agency performance against grant promises, and author grant reports.

Considerations for Raising Money through Special Events

Special events raise money through a combination of individual and business giving. Income is realized through ticket sales, event sponsorships, raffles, auctions, or ad journals. Gross revenues are generally high. However, the costs are also high. It generally costs fifty cents on the dollar to implement fundraising events, *not including labor*. And first-time event donors are unlikely to convert to repeat donors.

To implement a fundraising event, you will need a donor management system and a way to accept credit cards. Depending on the type of event, other costs may include raffle tickets, invitations, decorations, auction items, food venue rental, advertising, photography, insurance, security, licenses, and bidding materials. The labor involved is huge. Depending on the event, you will need to develop sponsorship templates, garner auction items, track auction donations, monitor bidding, deal with dissatisfied bidders, research potential business sponsors, record the research, reach out to the contact, follow up with the contact, make the ask, monitor and record responses, record donations and their purpose, and write thank-you letters. If a foundation is contributing to the event, you will need to monitor agency performance against grant promises and write grant reports. Someone also needs to plan the event, negotiate with the venue, pick the menu, design the invitations, make sure you have enough postage, send out the invitations, advertise the event, recruit ticket buyers, implement the communication vehicles, track individual and sponsorship tickets, provide answers when potential event-goers have questions, record donor interactions, receive the donations, and refund donations if there's a problem. Depending on the event, you may also need to coordinate the seating chart, create the golf foursomes, or track the walk team members. In addition, you may need to coordinate with the media.

Considerations for Raising Money from Government Contracts

Government contracts can provide substantial funding for critical social programs. However, government funding is associated with a bevy of risks.

The most direct threat to governmental funding is budget cuts. Budget cuts mean a reduction in the number or dollar amount of government contracts. Current funding may be reduced, new money may not be available, or there may be a complete elimination of funding. At any time during the application or renewal process, your contract may be subject to changes in budget allocations. In other words, the funding may be significantly delayed once you are approved for it. If the allocations are eliminated, you may not get the funding, even if you have been approved for it.

If the funding is delayed, it may cause cash flow problems. Unless you cease program operations until funding is received. Which causes other problems, like your clients not receiving needed services. If you stopped operations to deal with cash flow until funding is restored, you would still be required to meet your original program objectives. Most governmental contracts do not start until the date budget negotiations are over. The contract starts at the beginning of the federal, state, or local fiscal year, not the date funding is received. Relying on government funding is a gamble.

If you do pursue government grants, pay attention to how much the program is going to cost you to run. The allowable administrative expenses are very often lower than actual administrative expenses.

Make sure you know *all* the requirements for applying for the grant, operating the program, reporting program results, and reporting financial results. Government regulations are stringent and governmental monitoring can be onerous. Also, make sure that you have enough money to meet any match requirements. If the contract is going to cost more than you will receive, don't apply. If you still apply, have a solid plan in place for covering uncovered expenses.

You will also incur non-reimbursable preparation costs, mainly labor. Government grants are time-intensive to prepare and have complex application requirements. It costs staff time to attend mandatory technical assistance sessions. Also, government funding is so competitive that you may need to hire an expert to advise you in the process. Beware, though: your upfront costs are not reimbursable.

Governmental funding may be a good idea. Or, after assessment of the costs and risks, it may not.

Choosing your Fundraising Strategy

The steps to developing a fundraising strategy that will make you the most money are:

◆ Examine your fundraising costs and reduce expenses where you can, which is the least expensive and most immediate way to increase net income.

◆ Calculate your donor retention rate and try to improve it.

◆ Consider ways to increase your average donor gift.

◆ Research which fundraising techniques will bring you the highest net revenues.

◆ Explore which fundraising techniques will bring you the highest number of donations.

◆ Account for upfront and ongoing costs.

◆ Recruit new donors.

The biggest part of the charitable giving pie is through individuals, followed by foundations, then the business community. The return on investment is highest through foundation funding, followed by individual gifts from current donors, business giving, and new donor acquisition.

The costs of raising money through special events are high. Government funding can be undependable. When you create your fundraising plan, consider your return on investment. Remember, it's net, not gross, income that counts.

Wrapping It Up

◆ Look at your fundraising activities, including upfront revenues and expenses.

◆ Consider the return on investment of each activity.

◆ Analyze your fundraising performance, including donor volume.

◆ Analyze your financial performance, including labor costs.

◆ Weigh the costs and benefits of each activity.

Chapter Three

Understanding and Reaching Individual Donors

D ifferent fundraising techniques appeal to different generational cohorts. Segmenting your donors into age groups, researching age cohorts, and using the information to develop specific fundraising techniques that appeal to each generational group can drastically improve your fundraising results. The US Census Bureau and The Center for Generational Kinetics both proffer generational cohort information. You can use this information to create effective strategies that result in improved fundraising performance.

Mature Donors

At the time of writing, "the matures" is the oldest generational cohort alive, born 1945 or earlier. These people lived through the Great Depression and/or World War II when money was tight, and resources to meet everyday needs were rationed. Having to rely on themselves to make up for what was lacking, they became extraordinarily self-sufficient and thrifty. They pride themselves on being able to take care of their own needs and not asking for help. They also tend to scrutinize spending habits and be critical of extravagance and waste.

According to the "Charitable Giving in the USA 2019" report, the matures represent 26 percent of the country's total charitable giving. Fifty-two percent of them donate and 24 percent volunteer. According to "The Next Generation of American Giving: The Charitable Habits of Generation Z, millennials, Generation X, Baby Boomers, and Matures," by the Blackbaud Institute, top causes for mature donors include emergency relief, troops and veterans, the arts, advocacy, and election campaigns. Seventy-two percent donate in-kind goods and services. Mature donors prefer voice calls and direct mail; however, 30 percent give online. Most of them do not respond to text messaging or follow social media.

If you want to communicate with matures, do so through direct mail or phone. Email campaigns are iffy, including email newsletters. Mature donors probably won't view an online video either. Also, don't expect them to follow you or pay attention to what's happening on social media. If you find outliers, great! Remember, we're talking general preferences here.

Because thriftiness is such a critical value, mature donors may appreciate communications that talk about your agency's efforts at saving money, say through community partnerships that result in lower costs or partnerships that give value to clients above and beyond what your agency does. Because they also value self-sufficiency, matures may contribute to activities that encourage self-sustainability, either for your service recipients or your organization. If you ask for tangible things, or in-kind donations, you are likely to get them. For example, a fundraising campaign can contain an appeal for canned goods, gently used coats, or children's books, to name a few. Mature donors are also likely to be interested in receiving periodic financial updates.

Remember that matures are part of an aging cohort with probable health or mobility issues. If you want them to visit your agency or attend an event, make sure the facility is physically accessible. If your facility is not physically accessible, make it a priority to become so. (Do I hear a fundraising campaign in the making?) If you are offering food, make sure that your food choices are compatible with their dietary needs. Send the message, "You are important to us. We care about you as a person, not just a donor." If you put effort into your meeting donors' needs when they interact with you, they are more likely to continue interactions with you.

Baby Boomer Donors

Baby boomers were born from 1946 to 1964. Their parents fought in World War I, World War II, or the Korean Conflict. They fought in the Vietnam War, the Gulf Wars, and wars in Afghanistan and the Middle East. Baby boomers were shaped by a world rife with violent conflict. They yearn for communal peace and parity. That longing was intensified by the intense strife during the Civil Rights Movement and efforts to end the Vietnam War. Watergate further eroded confidence in the political establishment. The baby boomers' quest is a quest for social justice, human equity, and social harmony.

And they know how to get it. Baby boomers banded together, demanded civil rights legislation, and got it. They also brought an end to the Vietnam

War. Baby boomers believe in the power of community activism to change the world. They also believe in the power of young people to make those changes.

According to the "Charitable Giving in the USA 2019," 52 percent of baby boomers donate and 26 percent volunteer. They contribute a whopping 43 percent of all charitable giving. According to "The Next Generation of American Giving: The Charitable Habits of Generation Z, Millennials, Generation X, Baby Boomers, and Matures," baby boomer donors are top supporters of first responder organizations, human rights, religious, and spiritual causes. Fifty-eight percent of them will attend or participate in a fundraising event. Forty-nine percent of them give through a monthly giving program. Forty-six percent give through workplace initiatives. Twenty-one percent give through Facebook.

Baby boomer donors answer voice calls, email, text messaging, and direct mail. Twenty-four percent of baby boomer donors were promoted to online giving because of a direct mail appeal. Baby boomers are also active on social media.

Baby boomer donors, like mature donors, respond to direct mail and phone fundraising campaigns. Unlike matures, baby boomers will respond to email campaigns, text messages, and social media campaigns, primarily through Facebook. This means you have a lot of flexibility in designing and implementing your baby boomer donor communication vehicles. Baby boomers will read newsletters, view videos, and donate online. Tapping into their yearning for community betterment and promotion of social good, they will also like, follow, or promote nonprofits and their causes.

Whereas strong self-sufficiency messages will resonate best mature donors, strong messaging alluding to increasing the community good though activism will resonate best with baby boomers. Appeal to their sense of social equity and social justice in your fundraising campaigns. Talk to them in language that underlines how they are being active in communal efforts toward improving the human condition. Focus on collaborative organizational efforts.

And don't just ask for money. Ask baby boomers to participate in your agency's advocacy efforts. Advocacy feeds into baby boomers' sense of contribution to a common cause to increase social good. Use the baby boomers' willingness to like, follow, and promote your nonprofit and its mission.

Gen X Donors

Gen Xers were born 1965 to 1979. They are the sons and daughters of the early baby boomers. Gen Xers were born during periods of tremendous cultural turmoil: the civil rights era, Vietnam War protests, and the Watergate scandal. Women started working outside the home in higher numbers than before. With both parents working, many Gen Xers were latchkey kids. As latchkey children, they learned to rely on themselves to meet their own needs absent a caregiver. During that time, divorce rates went up, which gave rise to more single-parent and, when remarriage occurred, stepfamily arrangements.

Gen Xers came of age during the advent of computers and the rise in technology, which has had a tremendous impact on the way they communicate and interact. Gen Xers today tend to be established in their career paths with stable incomes. They also tend to be married with children in high school or college or living at home after college. As baby boomers retire, Gen Xers are taking their place as the movers and shakers in the workplace.

According to "Charitable Giving in the USA 2019," 57 percent of Gen Xers donate and 29 percent volunteer. They contribute 20 percent of all charitable giving. According to "The Next Generation of American Giving: The Charitable Habits of Generation Z, Millennials, Generation X, Baby Boomers, and Matures," top Gen X causes include health services, animal welfare, and environmental protection. Fifty-six percent will attend or participate in a fundraising event. Forty-nine percent donate through a monthly giving program. Nineteen percent give through Facebook. Gen Xers also respond to text messaging, email, social media, and phone calls.

Unlike mature donors, Gen X donors tend not to respond to direct mail appeals. Like the matures and baby boomers, Gen X donors will respond to phone calls. However, because of the rise of technology, the best way to reach Gen Xers is through email campaigns, text messaging, and social media. Whereas matures and baby boomers are more likely to rely on printed annual reports and financial statements to research nonprofits, Gen X donors tend to conduct due diligence using technology. Which means that the design and friendliness of your agency's website are of the utmost importance, including being mobile-friendly. If you haven't yet, make sure your website is mobile-friendly. You can also reach Gen X donors through online videos.

Much like with mature donors, when you craft your messages to Gen X donors, center them around themes of individualism and resourcefulness. Because they value self-sufficiency, Gen Xers may contribute to activities that encourage independence for your clients or your organization. Also, point out what makes your agency unique, not only in terms of mission fulfillment but also in the processes you use to meet your agency's mission. For example, talk about unique partnerships that leverage resources.

Millennial Donors

Millennials were born from 1980 to 1995. They are the sons and daughters of the later-born baby boomers. Unlike baby boomers, millennials did not grow up amidst cultural strife. They grew up with colossal advances in technology, including the advent of the Internet. They are incredibly tech-savvy. In fact, they take technology for granted. They don't know a world without it.

Millennials grew up participating in group activities, including playgroups, dance classes, and team sports, among others. They value teamwork. They look for ways to be included and involved. Growing up in a team environment where attainment of any kind was rewarded, millennials seek constant affirmation from others. They also tend to be committed, confident, and achievement-oriented.

Many millennials attended college and now carry high student loan debt. They tend to be married or in a relationship. If they have them, their children are preschool or elementary-school aged. Millennials juggle jobs with heavy family commitments, particularly for their children who tend to be involved in a multitude of after-school sports, music, and other activities.

According to "Charitable Giving in the USA 2019," 30 percent of millennials donate to nonprofit causes while 24 percent volunteer. They make up 11 percent of total charitable giving. According to "The Next Generation of American Giving: The Charitable Habits of Generation Z, Millennials, Generation X, Baby Boomers, and Matures," millennial donors are top supporters of human rights, international development, child development, and victims of crime and abuse. Fifty-five percent of millennial donors will attend or participate in a fundraising event. Forty percent of them donate through a monthly giving program. Forty-seven percent of them give through a website, while 16 percent give through Facebook. Millennial donors respond best to text messaging and social media, rarely responding to email or voice calls.

As opposed to mature and baby boomer donors who will respond to printed materials, millennial donors overwhelmingly respond to social media and text messaging. With millennials technology rules. The good news is that: 1) social media campaigns are less expensive and less labor-intensive than print and phone campaigns, and 2) all other donor groups except the majority of the matures will respond to social media.

Create campaigns that include viewing online videos; liking, following or promoting your nonprofit; participating in your cause; and donating to your organization. Of course, if you're asking people to give online, you need to make sure it is easy to find you. Where do you rank in Google searches? Do you provide links to your website in your electronic communications? What about your landing page? Make sure the site is up-to-date and appealing. Also, you need to make sure it is easy to give to you. Go through your process for making donations and count the clicks. Will a potential donor get frustrated and give up? Can your donation process be streamlined?

Millennials, like baby boomers, have a deep sense of social commitment. They are dedicated to social causes and committed to achieving positive social outcomes. Use advocacy campaigns and events to attract millennials to your cause. Emphasize the group nature of your campaigns. Plan group activities where team members can interact with one another, like community rallies or online petitions. Talk about how they can contribute to the team. Confident and team-oriented, millennials view themselves as equals to other team members. Play up that equality.

Thank-you messages are especially important to send to your millennial donors. Remember that, as a group, they need constant feedback and affirmation. Give it to them. Acknowledge *all* the contributions they make to your cause, not only monetary ones. Constantly validate them. Affirm their giving activities at *every* step.

If you want to engage your millennial donors further, plan short volunteer engagements or activities. Millennials don't have much time apart from tending to family commitments. Meeting their family commitments is extremely important to millennial donors. And they have young children involved in a variety of community activities. Structure your fundraising activities to be community events. Involve the whole family if you can.

Generation Z Donors

Generation Z, defined as people born after 1995, make up 25 percent of the US population. As a generation, they only know life during times of war: the September 11 terrorist attacks and the subsequent war on terrorism happened before they were born or when they were young children. They also live in a more diverse world than their previous generations: they grew up knowing an African American president. They will be the last white-majority generation in the United States. The Great Recession of 2008 also greatly affected Generation Z. Generation Z lived through the financial stresses of their parents, adopting attitudes of independence and autonomy similar to Gen Xers and the matures.

Moving beyond racial integration and women's movement of the baby boomers, Generation Z witnessed greater civil rights granted to the LGBTQ community. Their world is filled with hate crimes and mass shootings. Like the baby boomers, Generation Z sees the struggle between the old and the new in the context of political conflict. Political polarization currently dominates the current cultural struggle over how to deal with the rise of the minority-majority, the increase in mass shootings, and the acceptance of sexual fluidity. As a result, Generation Zers are politically active, even though most of them are not old enough to vote.

Wanting to win at everything, Generation Z is highly competitive. They want to get good grades, win at sports, be accepted into the best schools, and secure the highest paying jobs. To get ahead, they learn to act quickly before someone else beats them to the punch. Patience is not a strong suit. Neither is collaboration. As a result of their competitiveness, Generation Z tends to be independent, self-confident, and autonomous. Armed with ways to earn income through technology, Generation Zers are perfect young entrepreneurs.

Generation Z never knew a world without Facebook, Twitter, Tik Tok, WeChat, and Google. While millennial donors are technology savvy, Generation Z donors are technologically sophisticated. Twenty-five percent of Generation Z is always online. They also live on their mobile devices. Most of their information seeking and socialization is done through social media. In fact, they may prefer text messaging above face-to-face interactions.

Because limitless information has always been available at their fingertips, Generation Z donors form strong opinions about a broad array of topics. They are used to processing tremendous amounts of information in short bursts, resulting in eight-second-or-less attention spans. If you want their attention, you must grab it immediately.

Fifteen percent of Generation Z donates to charity. Twenty-six percent volunteer. They tend to be environmentally aware. Many of them are accumulating or saddled with high student loan debt.

The most effective thing you can do to improve your fundraising performance with Generation Z donors is to make sure your fundraising campaigns are accessible via mobile technology. Your website must be mobile-friendly. If you have not yet explored smartphone technologies, now is the time. Unlike baby boomers and Generation Xers, Generation Z will not respond to email. Like Gen X and millennial donors, Generation Z donors will respond to text messages. If you can create an app for giving to your organization, even better.

Effective fundraising campaigns targeted to Generation Z donors will employ short, quick, attention-grabbing communication techniques. Messages will be communicated through headlines, pictures, and captions.

Colors will be bold. Online videos will be brief, one, maybe two minutes at the most. Social media vehicles will include Twitter and Instagram to start. There are others.

In your messaging, describe what makes your organization the cream of the crop. Feature agency awards, testimonials, accreditations, and certifications in your communications. Pictures and logos are better than text. Use images that show diversity in gender, age, ethnicity, culture, and profession, among others.

Unlike millennial donors who respond to messages about collaboration, Generation Z donors respond to messages emphasizing independence and autonomy. And they are competitive. Design your fundraising campaigns to be competitive. Compare their individual giving against what they gave the year before or against the best giver in the class. Pit this year's income goal against last year's, making it a competition to see who topples the previous year's record. You can also pit their response against time. Ask for immediate responses while you have their eight seconds worth of attention. Come across as entrepreneurial and competitive as you can.

Generation Z donors are continually looking for new ideas and experiences. As with millennial donors, to successfully reach Generation Z donors, make your fundraising activities short with no long-term commitments. In addition, give your Generation Z donors opportunities to be heard and express their opinions. This means designing and structuring interactive communication and fundraising campaigns. Surveys are one way to elicit responses. Just make sure that if you ask for responses, you reply back. *Immediately.* The attention span of Generation Z donors is too short for anything else. Acknowledge them, thank them, validate them. Tell your Generation Z donors they are the best of the best.

Your individual donor base spans five generations. Know your donors inside and out. Use their preferred communication channels. Talk to them about things they are interested in ways that they will find satisfying. Ask them to do something. Give them a way to do it. And when they do it, reply back. Thank your donors. Report back to them. Dialogue with them. Interact with your donors in ways meaningful for them. Engage your donors. Let them engage with you. Build a successful donor relationship. And watch your fundraising results soar.

Wrapping It Up

To Effectively Reach Mature Donors:

- ◆ Direct mail and phone calls work.
- ◆ Print materials are preferred over electronic ones.
- ◆ Messages about frugality and resourcefulness are essential.
- ◆ Ask for in-kind donations, not only money.
- ◆ Self-sustenance is appealing.
- ◆ Physical accessibility is fundamental.
- ◆ Periodic financial updates are welcomed.

To Effectively Reach Baby Boomer Donors:

- ◆ Direct mail, phone calls, email campaigns, text messaging, and social media campaigns work.
- ◆ Vary the communication vehicles you use.
- ◆ Make your messages about social equity, social justice, and improving the human condition.
- ◆ Make donating to your cause an action that is part of a larger group effort.
- ◆ Ask for participation in advocacy efforts, not only money.
- ◆ Tap into workplace giving initiatives.

To Effectively Reach Gen X Donors:

- ◆ Email campaigns, text messaging, and social media campaigns work best.
- ◆ Ask them to like, follow, and promote you on social media.
- ◆ Craft your messages using themes of independence and resourcefulness.
- ◆ Tap into workplace giving initiatives.

To Effectively Reach Millennial Donors:

- ◆ Technology is where it's at. Liberally use social media and text messaging campaigns.
- ◆ Ask them to like, follow, and promote you on social media.
- ◆ Create messages emphasizing group accomplishments.
- ◆ Make donating to your cause an action that is part of a larger group effort.
- ◆ Ask for participation in advocacy efforts, not only money.

◆ Continually acknowledge, thank, and validate them.

◆ For maximum dollars, tap into workplace giving initiatives.

To Effectively Reach Generation Z Donors:

◆ Step up your social media and text messaging capabilities.

◆ Make sure your communications and website are mobile-friendly.

◆ Make messages short.

◆ Use attention-grabbing design.

◆ Diversity is important.

◆ Craft your messages using themes of independence and autonomy.

◆ Present yourself at the top of your game.

◆ Immediately reward them for responding to you.

Chapter Four

Making the Most of Your Grants Planning

According to *Giving USA,* foundations account for 18 percent of the charitable dollar. And they tend to give more substantial, major gifts. If only you could find a way to get more grants. How do you find the time? What tools can you develop that will help you get those grants more easily?

Start by Visiting your Agency's Strategic Plan

A strategic plan contains your agency's mission, vision, and values statements, telling the reader your organization's purpose and guiding principles. The plan speaks to what community needs your agency meets and the programs and services in place to meet them. A strategic plan is the roadmap of how your agency will achieve its mission. It is crucial, in both researching available funding and writing the respective proposals, that you, as the grant professional, be familiar with your nonprofit's strategic plan.

Adhering to your agency's strategic plan will help you avoid mission drift. Mission drift occurs when agency resources are used for things other than mission, for example, a youth counseling agency implementing an after-school program, or a community food bank running a cooking school. The danger is that the after-school program or cooking school swallows up the respective counseling services or the food bank. You must be careful. Ancillary services may be complementary and feel like a natural fit. But if the ancillary programs replace your core services, you've lost your way. And foundations are keen to avoid that. Foundations like nonprofits that stick to their missions.

More and more foundations want to know if your agency has an updated strategic plan, particularly those foundations with bigger payouts. They want to know you are prepared for the future. Studies show that nonprofits who have written strategic plans realize better results, including fundraising results, than those without a written plan.

The values stated in the strategic plan can be used to improve your fundraising performance, steering you in the direction of who to ask for funding. Only apply to foundations that share your values. For example, is your health and wellness nonprofit really going to accept an award from a tobacco firm? If you did, what kind of message does that send to your clients? To your other funders? To your community?

The strategic plan also gives you the information you need to write your grant narratives. Depending on how comprehensive your agency's strategic plan is, you may have the start of your proposal's community needs assessment, organizational description, and sustainability plan already written.

Then Look at Your Agency's Chart of Accounts

We cannot tell you how many times we have seen good programs get funded, but the agency still financially failed, because the grant budget did not include all the costs necessary to run the program. To maintain the financial health of your agency, it is imperative that your total program costs are covered, not only the direct costs associated with program operations. When you don't ask for enough money, you can run at a deficit and not know it. You may, by looking at the revenue coming in, think that you are doing well when, in actuality, you are doing more harm than good. Your nonprofit's chart of accounts will list all the line item expenses you need to consider when crafting your proposal's budget. Always use a chart of accounts to know what line items to include in the grants budget so that the organization stays solvent.

What about when line items in my chart of accounts aren't allowed by the foundation? Well, then you have line items that you can include as part of your agency's contribution to the program. And you know you need to find other funding, maybe through your other fundraising activities. Which helps the sustainability piece in your narrative. A variety of fundraising methods shows a diversified portfolio. Also, a multitude of donors shows broad community support, which helps your background, or credibility, narrative.

Ask your agency bookkeeper, accountant, or financial officer for your organization's chart of accounts. Make sure you present who—whether the foundation, you, or someone else—will pay for all the costs associated with the program described in your proposal.

Next Develop a Master Narrative

Developing a master grant narrative does *not* mean writing a grant proposal that you use and reuse, slapping on different contact mailing information. Developing a master narrative means that for each program your agency runs, you develop a comprehensive document that can be used for the various proposals you will write. You are writing a master document that you have at hand that can be customized for each grant submission.

In your master narrative, answer the questions related to why your nonprofit is doing what it is doing, where it's doing it, and what makes it uniquely qualified to do it. Answer the questions: Why this community as opposed to others? Why these clients and not others? Why this strategy instead of that one? Why these programs and not those? Why do your clients come to your organization and not go somewhere else? Why do community partners collaborate with you and not someone else? What makes you stand out above other of your kind? You want to thoroughly the question foundations will have, "Why should we fund your program as opposed to the hundreds of others that we're looking at?"

What kind of data supports your argument of why you're the best? To fully answer the question, you need community, client, and staff data. You need organizational, financial, and community partnership data. You need program data, including history, processes and procedures, outcomes, evaluations, costs, and financial performance. Sometimes you need data on governance structure and processes. Some funders, usually corporate foundations, request market and branding data, public relations processes and outcomes, and asset and debt information. In government grants, you may also need legislative data. For your master document, get as much data as you can. Research, research, research. Document, document, document. The more objective data you have that supports your arguments for different types of funding, the better off you are.

Craft a narrative for each program for which you will write for funding. Go-to narratives save you time in research, helping you find time to write a greater number of grants. Referring to the master document will also help you maintain consistency between all your grant narratives. Consistency is vital because foundation officers talk to one another, and you want to maintain a steady reputation and unified organizational identity. More detailed information on how to write successful grant proposals is available through the Nonprofit Quick Guide *How to Answer the Eight Questions Every Grant Reviewer Asks.*

Now Research Foundations

As we talked about in the Nonprofit Quick Guide *How to Find New Donors and Get Them to Give to Again*, it is best to go through foundations' IRS Form 990s to do your research on them. The 990s are chock full of information about the mission, contact information, application procedures, and who they have funded for what in what amount. Nothing beats a 990 for details on potential foundation funders.

To easily get through all the returns, you may want to invest in a good foundation database. There are several out there. Foundation Search and Foundation Directory Online are two. A search database allows you to segment information based on foundation issues of interest, geographic areas, and others. You can also weed out those foundations who do not accept unsolicited proposals. A foundation database gives you summary information that you can drill down on and confirm in the attached 990. You can also find 990s on GuideStar.

Once you have the 990 information, go to the foundations' websites. Look for any information that disqualifies you as a good fit for them. For example, if a foundation gives to biodiversity, it funds only zoos; that is not a fit if your organization is a botanical garden. Or if it gives to education, specifically university research, it won't be a fit if your organization is an after-school program. The last thing you want to do is waste your time writing a grant proposal that doesn't have a chance of being funded. You are too busy for that. Also, you don't want your organization to get a bad reputation. Foundation funders are a pretty small group that tend to network with one another. You don't want to be known as the nonprofit that doesn't do its homework.

By visiting its website, you are also looking for clues as to how the foundation talks about issues: how it categorizes information and what values are important to it. Visit every page on its website. Read its annual reports and white papers, if it has them. Look for clues on how you might write your proposal narratives so that its program officers and board members best relate to them. You want your nonprofit's mission to match its mission. You want similar organizational values. You want your information to be categorized in the same way its information is. You want to use some of the same words and concepts it does. You want to come across as understandable and relatable as you can.

After you have looked at its 990 and visited its website, if a foundation is a good match and it allows it, call the program officer. Confirm your interpretations of the material it has provided. Ask questions. Make a memorable impression. You want that program officer to remember you as asking intelligent questions when the funding decisions are being made. You want to submit the best proposal you can.

Finally, Record Information, Create a Calendar, and Track Progress

Whether you use a commercial donor database or an Excel sheet, you need to record the information you have gathered. You, of course, want the name and contact information of the foundation, the foundation's areas of interest, the type of funding it awards (program, seed money, general operating, equipment, etc.), and the range of funding it gives.

Knowing the range of funding is not enough, though. Sometimes those ranges are $250 to $2.5 million. You need to know the appropriate amount you should ask for. You find that amount by going through the foundation 990s list of funded programs, finding those similar to yours, and seeing the typical amounts given toward them. Look at several years' worth of giving data. You want to know whether it is a one-time funder or a foundation that likes to build relationships and award increasing amounts over the years.

You will want all this information in a summary format so that you can easily see when submissions are due, proposals are submitted, awards are received, thank-you letters are sent, payments are received, and reports are due. And you want to be able to sort that information both by the name of the foundation and due date. You want to sort by foundation name so you can see the foundation's history with your organization. You want to sort by the due date so that you have a ready-made calendar.

If you can afford an electronic donor database, whether software-based on online service, get it. It will save you time and might be able to be integrated into your accounting software. But if you don't have the budget for one, an Excel sheet can suffice.

For years I used an Excel sheet. It looked something like this:

Due Date	Date Submitted	Foundation Name	Funding Areas	Funding Type	Request Amount	Date Awarded	Amount Awarded	Date Received	Thank-You Sent	Notes

Do you want to realize more grant income next year than you have this year? Be familiar with your nonprofit's strategic plan. Look at the chart of accounts to ensure that total costs are covered. Maximize your time by creating a master narrative and creating a master calendar. Increase your chances of funding by writing an easily understandable and relatable proposal.

Wrapping It Up

◆ Use your agency's strategic plan as a guide for your grant writing efforts.

◆ Make sure to present total costs in your grant budgets.

◆ Develop a master case for support that can be used to customize your grant submissions.

◆ Research potential foundation prospects' IRS Form 990s, websites, annual reports, and white papers and then contact program officers.

◆ Use a database or Excel sheet to record information, create a grants calendar, and track progress.

Chapter Five

Getting the Most Out of Business Contributions

Unlike foundations, businesses are not obligated to give away money. Business owners want to make money. Corporations are accountable to stockholders who demand they make money. Never forget, no matter how charitable they may be, business donors have skin in the game because they believe their relationship with you will result in higher profits. So how does a mission-oriented, socially accountable nonprofit help a for-profit business increase its profits?

As we learned in the Nonprofit Quick Guide *How to Find New Donors and Get Them to Give to Again*, the first and easiest way to increase your business donors' profits is by exposing them to new customers. You can give them exposure through a well-publicized fundraising event, newsletter, press release, website, or social media post, to name a few. Businesses are also keenly interested in their reputations in the community. Companies can enhance their reputations by partnering with impactful nonprofits, which ultimately helps sales, a for-profit's primary objective.

Business donors are also interested in decreasing their costs, including advertising and personnel costs. Recent studies have shown that a reputation for doing good in the community leads to lower employee recruitment and retention costs. As a result, companies offer employee giving matching gift programs, employee volunteer opportunities, and employee donor advised funds. Employee volunteer opportunities are a good way for a business to reduce its employee training costs as employees can learn and practice many leadership and team-building skills while volunteering.

Companies may also be looking for opportunities to access to legislators and governmental regulators. Are legislators and government officials invited to your events? What other networking opportunities can your nonprofit offer business executives to access the regulators they want to influence?

Baby Boomers and the Workplace

Baby boomers represent 25 percent of the US workforce. As we saw in **Chapter Four**, baby boomers are interested in social good. To attract and retain them, businesses today engage heavily in social responsibility initiatives. Companies offer many workforce giving programs, including employee matching gifts, employee volunteerism, and management of employee donor advised funds. Do you know who employs your baby boomer donors? Do you encourage your donors to look into employer matching gift programs? What about volunteer programs? Tap into baby boomer workers. Forty-six percent of baby boomer donors give through workplace initiatives.

Gen Xers and the Workplace

At 33 percent, Gen Xers make up a significant portion of the US workforce. This means that just like baby boomer workers, companies are eager to recruit and retain them. Do you know who your Gen X donor employers are? Have you asked them? Do you promote employer matching gift programs? Does your organization recruit or have a base of Gen X volunteers? Do their employers pay them for the volunteerism or make contributions on their behalf when they volunteer? Have you talked to the decision-makers of the corporate philanthropy efforts to find out if your cause falls into company giving areas? Letting your Gen X donors know you do these things shows resourcefulness, which may appeal to them, possibly increasing the number or amount of their donations.

Millennials and the Workplace

Millennials are a potent force in the corporate world, making up 33 percent of the workforce. Who employs your millennial donors? Will those employers pay you or their employees for volunteer experiences? Do you promote employer matching gift programs, letting your millennial donors know your nonprofit partners with their company? Letting your millennial donors know your nonprofit collaborates with other community entities shows those donors they are part of powerful, effective teams making progress toward achieving social good, which may increase the amount or frequency of their donations.

No matter how philanthropic they are, business motivations for charitable giving include the quest for profits through increased sales, bettering their reputation, or reducing costs. To recruit and retain workers, businesses offer a variety of workforce giving programs, including employee matching gifts, employee volunteerism, and management of employee donor advised funds. Take advantage of all of them.

Wrapping It Up

◆ Never forget business donors have skin in the game because they believe their relationship with you will result in higher profits.

◆ Appeal to baby boomers, Gen Xers, and millennials when designing your strategy to reach the business community.

◆ Businesses, eager to attract and retain talent, invest in a variety of social responsibility vehicles, including employee matching gifts, employee volunteerism, and management of employee donor advised funds.

Chapter Six

Planning for the Success of Your Nonprofit Fundraising Events: Income, Impact, Costs, and Benefits

How do your agency's fundraising events fare? Are they related to your nonprofit's mission? Do they raise a lot of money? Really? At what cost, the human effort included? What kind of impact do your events make? Is the community galvanized to spread your agency's message? In terms of mission fulfillment, net income, and community impact, how do your events really fare?

The Importance of Designing and Implementing Mission-Related Fundraising Events

As we discussed in the Nonprofit Quick Guide *How to Find New Donors and Get Them to Give to Again*, people are motivated to give because of your nonprofit's impactful mission, not your agency's need for money. Yes, donors might attend an event because they've been asked in a quid pro quo relationship to attend, that is, you come to my event, and I'll go to yours. But you don't get dedicated, engaged donors out of quid pro quo interactions. Research shows that attendees of fundraising events generally do not convert to repeat donors. If attendees are at your event because they feel obligated, you've just gone through a lot of time and effort to get a one-time donation. That's an expensive way to raise funds.

You raise money to fulfill the mission. So, invite guests who are interested in solving the community issue you address. Design the event with mission fulfillment in mind. Let your ambassadors talk about why they are involved with your agency. Make it easy for your ambassadors to speak with passion about your mission. You will realize better long-term fundraising results. It is mission that motivates. It is mission fulfillment that spurs giving.

Don't chase the money. Once you start chasing money, mission drift starts to occur. Mission drift, focusing on activities other than your mission, is a dangerous thing. And it generally occurs slowly. Does this event that you're planning have anything to do with mission fulfillment? If it doesn't, don't do it. Err on the side of caution. Don't be tempted by the lure of easy money. The costs are too high. Once mission drift starts, you begin to lose community support. The gain of a dollar today is not worth the lack of community support tomorrow. It's a matter of short-term versus long-term gain. Both must be taken into account when you evaluate the success of your events.

So, your fundraising events are mission-infused. Now, do they actually make money?

Evaluating Income Generated through Successful Fundraising Events

The amount of gross income you raise is one way to measure your success. Gross income is the way fundraisers most often describe the success of their events. For example, *our gala raised $100,000.*

Gross income means nothing, though. As we saw in **Chapter One**, it is net, not gross, income that counts when determining successful fundraising performance. If you raised $100,000 in gross revenues, but it took $125,000 to raise it, you just lost money. The lure is, and why so many boards and executive directors are prone to think fundraising events raise a lot of money, is they think in terms of gross, rather than net, income.

If you are in line with the average industry return, your event expenses should be no more than half of your gross revenue. In other words, if you raised $100,000 through your fundraising event, your direct event costs should be no more than $50,000. Accounting for your events' direct event expenses, how much money do your events make?

But it's not enough to stop there. To know if you really made money on an event, you need to account for total, not only direct, costs. What happens to your net income when you add labor costs and allocate a portion of your general and administrative expenses?

Are you breaking even now? Great, if your objectives for the event were things other than making money, like community goodwill, community visibility, or strengthening of strategic partnerships. Which are noble purposes for events. One of the outcomes of good events is community awareness and mobilization. In that case, a break-even return is okay.

You've accomplished what you set out to do, and you haven't lost money doing it. These are often referred to as friend-raising, as opposed to fundraising, events. If you implemented a friend-raising event and broke even, good job. But be sure everyone is aware of the goals of the event before you plan it—is a fundraising event or a friend-raiser? It doesn't become a friend-raising event only after you realize you lost money!

Did you lose money after you account for the labor and overhead costs? If you're like most nonprofits, your organization's fundraising events lost money. Is that something you can afford? If you don't want to lose money, the event isn't worth doing again, unless you make some changes so that it at least breaks even.

Evaluating Impact When Evaluating Fundraising Event Performance

In addition to evaluating mission fulfillment and net income, you can measure the success of your events in terms of impact. How much of a lasting community awareness did your events make? Did your events build strategic relationships? Do participants look forward to the events? Do guests have a good time? Will they come again? What about event organizers? How much do they look forward to the event? Do you lose volunteers or drain staff by putting on this event? What do negative experiences do to your agency's ambassadors' ability to communicate positive, passionate messages about your organization? What was the true impact of your event?

Accounting for Opportunity Costs When Evaluating Fundraising Event Performance

Finally, you need to look at the opportunity costs associated with implementing your events, that is, the costs you incurred by *not* doing something else. Did your events prevent you from doing other things that would bring you a higher return on your efforts? As mentioned earlier, it typically costs about fifty cents, not counting labor and overhead, to raise a dollar through fundraising events. Are there other fundraising vehicles that will bring you greater returns on your dollar, be more mission infused, and create a more significant impact? Opportunity costs are worth evaluating as part of your overall fundraising event performance.

Analyzing the success of your nonprofit fundraising events includes evaluating your events in terms of the amount of mission focus, positive net income, and community awareness and mobilization the event achieves. Make your fundraising as mission infused, profitable, and impactful as you can.

Wrapping It Up

Results	Analysis
Low Mission Low Income Low Impact	And you do this because…?
Low Mission Low Income High Impact	You've spent money to drift from your mission, and everyone doesn't know what you do—reinvent the event.
Low Mission High Income Low Impact	You've made money but watch out! You're in danger of mission drift and losing credibility in the community. Add mission.
Low Mission High Income High Impact	You've accomplished financial and impact goals, but no one knows why—add mission and watch for mission drift.
High Mission Low Income Low Impact	You're getting there—you've just spent money on fulfilling mission. Cut costs to increase income and let people know about your mission by adding impact to the event.
High Mission Low Income High Impact	You're almost there—fulfilling your mission and increasing community support. Now cut costs to realize higher income.
High Mission High Income Low Impact	You've accomplished fulfilling and raising money for your mission. All you need to do to be perfect is to add impact.
High Mission High Income High Impact	Congratulations—you're the envy of every fundraiser! You've got a winner!!!!

Chapter Seven

Creating a Profitable Nonprofit Fundraising Budget and Calendar

Yes, you *can* realize a "profit" as a nonprofit, technically not really a profit so much as a net surplus. Nonprofit is a tax classification, not a business plan. A nonprofit, as opposed to a for-profit, is not allowed to give the profits to business owners or corporate stockholders. A nonprofit *can* make a profit. The profits just need to be directed toward fulfilling the mission, as opposed to individual business owners.

You need three things to create a profitable fundraising strategy:

1. Strict adherence to mission;
2. Revenue-generating activities that make more than they cost; and
3. A lens that will help choose among the numerous fundraising options available.

Creating a Profitable Nonprofit Fundraising Budget and Calendar: Step One

Fundraising is not about the money. It is mission that motivates. Individuals are looking for mission fulfillment. Foundations are looking for mission fulfillment. Businesses are looking for a strong sense of corporate identity, which, for a nonprofit, is mission fulfillment. Make sure the fundraising activities you choose help you fulfill your mission. Don't chase after the money.

As stated in **Chapter Five**, chasing after the money can lead to mission drift. If your organization experiences mission drift, eventually you will lose your community support. Individual donors won't know what you stand for, you will not meet foundation requirements for mission fulfillment, and businesses will pick up on your weak organizational identity.

Practically speaking, sticking to your mission means asking and thanking your donors for how they impact community, not financial, needs. It means researching grants with similar missions as opposed to big payouts. It means choosing special events that are designed to fulfill mission just as much as raise money. Does that run or golf tournament or casino night have anything to do with your organization's mission? *Always* stay true to your organization's mission.

In addition to mission, stay true to your nonprofit's organizational values. Is whatever activity in which you are engaging in line with those values? Do you know what your nonprofit's values are? No? Then go to the strategic plan and find out. Do you *not* have value statements? Then work with your board and develop them. Value statements will help you define your nonprofit's identity and choose good financial partners.

A precise identity leads to increased donations. By making your values known and using them as a guide to fundraising, your individual donors will connect with you at a deeper level and, when they are asked to give at a sacrificial level, they are more likely to do so. Your agency's values can also help you determine which foundations to apply to. Are your organizational values compatible with their missions? If they are, the foundation may be worth exploring as a source for funding. If they are not, move on to the next prospect. What about your business donors? Does your organization share values with them? If you do and you have a strong sense of who you are and what you stand for, your nonprofit is going to be an attractive potential partner to them. Companies spend millions of dollars defining who they are and what they stand for. It's called branding. It is good for businesses to establish a strong brand. Strong branding increases business profits. The same is true of nonprofits.

Creating a Profitable Nonprofit Fundraising Budget and Calendar: Step Two

Without mission, there is no money, and without money, there is no mission. After making sure your fundraising activities are mission-related, the next step is to evaluate them in terms of profitability. You need to make an overall profit, so your agency has emergency reserves and seed money for new projects. Setting aside a portion of profits is how these things get funded.

What are your revenues and expenses for each activity? Not just your direct expenses, your indirect ones too. Like fundraising staff salaries, database costs, professional memberships, trade publications, and professional development costs. Also include executive management, accounting, human resource, and IT allocations. And rent, utility, and office supply apportionments. Analyze each fundraising activity— writing grants, making direct appeals, asking for major gifts, bidding on government contracts, executing fundraising events—as if it is a separate business center. Treat each one as a stand-alone activity. Which ones made you money? You might want to repeat them. Which ones cost you money? Unless you have another reason for doing them, you might not want to do them anymore, even if it is the favorite activity of the board or staff. The purpose of fundraising is, after all, to raise funds. You need to make money to thrive.

Creating a Profitable Nonprofit Fundraising Budget and Calendar: Step Three

Once you look at their mission and financial performance, some of your fundraising activities may not be working for you in the way you want them to. Maybe they are very mission-oriented, but you're losing money. Or perhaps they're making a ton of money but aren't related to your mission at all. Well, there's a third lens you need to look at your fundraising activities through: the impact lens. What kind of impact does the activity make?

For example, how much mission does that grant or government contract fulfill? Probably a lot. It might be worth it to you to subsidize any losses with other fundraising activities that are making you money. Or how much community awareness does that gala or walk generate? Maybe a lot. You might want to keep them, fill them with more mission orientation, and look at ways you can increase their revenues or reduce their expenses.

What are your other organizational impact goals? Do you want to create awareness? Do you want to recruit new donors? Do you want to provide for high-powered networking between government officials and major donors? Do you want your business donors to get to know your clients? Precisely what are your goals in terms of the impact you want to make through that particular fundraising activity? You might have a good reason to give up more tangible high profits for less tangible high impact.

By the way, there is no right or wrong answer. It all depends on the goals and annual objectives stated in your agency's strategic plan.

Creating a Profitable Nonprofit Fundraising Budget and Calendar: Step Four

Now that you've looked at each fundraising activity in terms of mission, profit, and impact, you need to compare the performance of the activities to one another. Comparing the activities to one another will help you determine how much time investment to make in each. There are many activities to choose from: you can write a grant, bid for an upcoming government contract, implement another fundraising event, help board members cultivate major donors, educate a politician about the needs of your clients and the impact legislative policies have on them, initiate an email campaign, or prepare a direct mailing. The list goes on. There are an infinite number of things you can do to raise money.

Face it. You and your team, be it staff or volunteers, have limited time. Time is your most precious commodity. The question is not, "How much can I do?" The question is, "What activities can I do more of that will bring me the most return on my investment? How can I shape my mix of fundraising activities so that they are the most profitable they can be?"

Don't only look at straight net income when you are comparing different fundraising activities. Look at net income in terms of the costs of the resources you invest in them. Divide net income by expenses for each fundraising activity. What are your results? Where is your highest return on investment? What activities do you do that bring in the most amount of money using the least amount of resources?

Maybe writing that extra grant delivers a higher return on investment than implementing that small fundraiser. Perhaps you find that soliciting major gifts is your highest return on investment, higher even than writing that grant. Maybe you find your Facebook campaign delivers your highest return on investment. Whatever it is, that's where you focus your resources when you have choices to make.

Creating a Profitable Nonprofit Fundraising Budget and Calendar: Step Five

Your activities are mission-oriented. You make money on them. You've evaluated their impact in terms of other organizational goals. And you are directing your resources where they will be most efficient. Now look at your calendar and start mapping out your activities.

Schedule the fundraising activities that are so central to mission and impact they must be done first. In some organizations, that may be a special event that brings together the community. In other agencies, it may be a direct appeal centered around a community-recognized theme, such as suicide prevention month or earth day. Whatever the fundraising activity, just make sure your costs are covered.

Since 30 percent of charitable giving takes place in the last quarter of the year, it makes sense to schedule a year-end appeal sometime during the last three months of the year. The second-highest giving season is in the spring, around tax time. If you want to be different, or you want to have two individual appeals during the year because appeals bring you the highest return on your investment, a spring appeal may be a good option for you.

Now, look at activities that have hard deadlines, usually your grant submissions and government contracts. Make a note of the deadlines and schedule time to write them.

You must also schedule time to cultivate, ask for, and steward major gifts if you want to realize maximum results. As we saw in **Chapter One**, the cost to raise a dollar through individual giving is much, much lower than through a fundraising event. Moreover, the donation is more likely to be repeated for a longer period than a grant. It can be more stable than government contracts, which are subject to the political whims of budget allocations. An undesignated major gift means you can use the money wherever it is most needed, including general operating expenses or infrastructure, which you often can't with grants or government contracts. Figure out how and when your organization is going to solicit major gift prospects and what you need to do to facilitate the process.

How many people do you want in your major gifts pipeline? "As many as possible" is not an acceptable answer. How many prospective major gift prospects can you realistically help board members to cultivate and still do everything else? Are you going to set aside a quarter to do a major gifts campaign, or are you going to have ongoing asks? Schedule the time and set the benchmarks, or it won't get done. What gets measured gets done.

Creating a Profitable Nonprofit Fundraising Budget and Calendar: Step Six

Finally, go to your organizational budget, plug in your development budget, and make sure you can maintain positive cash flow and not go into debt. Direct mail appeals and special events, in particular, usually cost more than other types of fundraising. Make sure you have enough money to purchase the needed supplies or secure the needed venues upfront, without going into debt. Fundraising performance is never guaranteed. A serve snowstorm, a hurricane, a city-wide blackout, a fire—you never know what may affect your fundraising performance. Manage your financial risks. Make sure you have enough cash on hand so that you can absorb the financial risks you are taking.

You need to be able to pay the bills. If you don't pay your bills, you will eventually go out of business. And you need to pay your bills without going into debt. You don't want to be financially desperate. Because when agencies start getting desperate about money, they start chasing the dollar as opposed to the mission. Mission drift starts. Community support declines. Employee morale declines. And the downward cycle has begun.

Long story short: Schedule and implement profitable, mission-oriented fundraising activities that make an impact and focus your resources so that they bring you the greatest financial return.

Wrapping It Up

◆ Put mission first.

◆ Ensure profitability.

◆ Make an impact.

◆ Implement activities where you get the best return on investment.

◆ Determine your schedule with community observances, fundraising cycles, and grant deadlines in mind.

◆ Make sure you maintain positive cash flow.

relatable proposal. Make sure your grant budgets include both direct and indirect costs. Walk away from grant funding that loses money, unless you have an overall plan for covering uncovered costs.

Never forget that business owners are interested in realizing profits. No matter how philanthropic they are, companies engage in relationships with nonprofits because they believe the relationships will directly or indirectly increase profits. Your nonprofit can help businesses achieve their goals by offering increased corporate visibility to your nonprofit agency constituencies, enhancing their reputation through association with your nonprofit's positive community impact, or reducing their business costs through your agency's advertising and volunteer opportunities. Your nonprofit can benefit from a myriad of workforce giving programs, including employee matching gifts, employee volunteerism, and management of employee donor advised funds.

Implementing fundraising events can be very time-intensive. Special event revenue may not be as much as you think. Include labor costs when you assess the financial success of your event. Evaluate the success of your events in terms of how much mission focus they achieve, the net income they raise, as well as the impact on the community, volunteers, and staff they make. Be willing to let go of a special event that isn't producing the results you desire.

Schedule and implement fundraising activities that bring you the greatest return on your investment. Ensure positive net income. Maintain a positive cash flow. Make a positive impact. Put mission first. Create a fundraising strategy that is as mission infused, operationally efficient, profitable, and impactful as it can be.

Chapter Eight

Bringing It All Together

So, what activities are the best ones to implement? It all depends on your nonprofit's goals.

To raise the most money, look at net as opposed to gross income. The least expensive and most immediate way to realize more income is by cutting costs. Also, examine your donor retention efforts, often the most cost-effective way to reduce overall fundraising costs. Consider reducing direct and operating fundraising costs if you can. However, don't cut costs that pay for themselves in terms of productivity.

The usual nonprofit fundraising strategies utilize individual giving, foundation requests, corporate contributions, special events, and government contracts. Each has its own costs and benefits. Research the financial costs and benefits of implementing each fundraising technique and weigh your results.

Your individual donor base spans five generations. To get maximum financial results, know the needs, perspectives, and preferences of each generational cohort. Design fundraising activities and communications that will best appeal to the age group you're trying to reach. Communicate with them from their unique perspectives. Then engage them. Ask them to do something apart from making a donation. Make sure it is easy for them to respond to you. When they respond, reply back. Thank them. Report the results of their efforts back to them. Start a dialogue. Build a successful two-way relationship.

When pursuing grant funding, let your agency's strategic plan be your guide. Know your agency's mission, values, goals, and roadmap. Match your mission and values with those of potential foundation funders. Maximize your time by creating a master narrative and creating a master calendar. Increase your chances of funding by writing an easily understandable and